MALE SPORTS STARS

DISC

IN THIS SERIES

Superstars of Men's Figure Skating

Superstars of Men's Pro Wrestling

Superstars of Men's Soccer

Superstars of Men's Swimming and Diving

Superstars of Men's Tennis

Superstars of Men's Track and Field

MALE SPORTS STARS

Superstars of Men's PRO WRESTLING

by Matt Hunter

CHELSEA HOUSE PUBLISHERS

Philadelphia

Produced by Choptank Syndicate, Inc.

Editor and Picture Researcher: Norman L. Macht
Production Coordinator and Editorial Assistant: Mary E. Hull
Design and Production: Lisa Hochstein
Cover Illustrator: Earl Parker

First Printing

1 3 5 7 9 8 6 4 2

Library of Congress Cataloging-in-Publication Data

Hunter, Matt
        Superstars of men's pro wrestling / Matt Hunter
            p.   cm.—(Male sports stars)
        Includes bibliographical references (p.) and index.
        Summary: Profiles wrestling's top performers, from Abdullah the Butcher
    and Andre the Giant to Hulk Hogan and Taz.
        ISBN 0-7910-4587-0
        1. Wrestlers—Biography—Juvenile literature. [1. Wrestlers.]
        I. Title. II. Series
    GV1196.H86 1998
    796.812'092273—dc21   97-50131
                                                               CIP
                                                                AC

CONTENTS

10/6/98 PXT 16.95

1 HOW IT ALL BEGAN

Wrestling is as old as mankind. Cavemen may have grappled with rivals for food or territory, and with animals for survival. The Bible contains references to the sport, and the tombs of the pharaohs in ancient Egypt bear carvings of wrestling contests from thousands of years ago. Greek mythology is also rich with legends of wrestling. The gods on Mount Olympus engaged in wrestling matches for sport and to determine supremacy. There is also evidence of wrestling activity in ancient Japan and India.

Wrestling's popularity grew when it was included in the original Olympic Games held in Greece nearly 3,000 years ago. Today wrestling remains one of the purest forms of competition— one person is pitted against another with no equipment other than sheer skill and wits.

The United States also has a wrestling tradition. George Washington, the first president of the U.S., was a top wrestler in the Virginia colony. While in school, he once defeated a state champion after only a few weeks of instruction and experience. Other presidents also excelled at wrestling. Abraham Lincoln was an accomplished wrestler who taught the sport to fellow soldiers when he served in the army. President William Howard Taft was a wrestling champion during his college days at Yale University.

The sport of wrestling as we know it today did not become organized until the late 1800s. The

Jackson, the valet, peels off the hair net, unleashing Gorgeous George's mane while the master busies himself with his fur-trimmed silk robe before a 1964 match.

Murals on the walls of Pharaoh Beni-Hasan's tomb in Egypt depict hundreds of wrestling scenes dating back to 1900 B.C.

first generally acknowledged Western champion of organized wrestling was George Hackenschmidt. After winning several tournaments in Germany, Italy, and England, Hackenschimdt defeated Tom Jenkins on May 5, 1904, in New York, becoming the wrestling champion of North America.

Professional wrestlers emphasized the technical skills of the sport during the first half of the twentieth century. They were athletes, not showmen. Early champions included Ed "Strangler" Lewis, Jim Londos, Everett Marshall, and Lou Thesz.

In the early 1950s, as television sets began appearing in people's homes, broadcasters found that viewers loved to watch wrestling. The small area of the wrestling ring in which the action took place was easily framed for the cameras and the small screens of early television sets. The first superstar of televised wrestling was "Gorgeous" George Wagner. He was like nothing wrestling had ever seen: an outrageous character who demanded that his valet spray the ring with perfume before he would climb through the ropes. He was also a preening egotist who hated to have his bleached-blond tresses mussed during the course of a match.

Gorgeous George was the wrestler everybody loved to hate. He became a leading box office attraction, earning an estimated $2 million in his career—a lot of money for the 1950s. His bragging and posturing were an immense success, and Gorgeous George set the pace for almost every wrestler who followed him.

On November 7, 1962, Gorgeous George bet his flowing mane against the unmasking of

This ancient piece of Greek pottery depicts two wrestlers. Wrestling was included in the original Olympic Games, which took place in Greece nearly 3,000 years ago.

The Destroyer in Los Angeles. The Destroyer won, and George was shaved completely bald. In 1963, at the age of 48, Gorgeous George died of a heart attack in his Hollywood apartment. More than anyone else, he moved wrestling across the line from sport to entertainment. The bond between television and wrestling has remained rock solid ever since.

LEGENDS OF THE SQUARED CIRCLE

Many colorful wrestling superstars have helped to shape the modern wrestling scene. Nobody was ever better as the vicious villain than Abdullah the Butcher. Standing 6' 1" and weighing 360 blubbery pounds, Abdullah was no athlete. But behind his vicious appearance, he possessed some wrestling skills, including an excellent elbow drop. In the three decades after his 1958 pro debut, Abdullah, a native of the Sudan, set a standard for bloodthirsty brutality that simultaneously fascinated and disgusted fans around the world. When Abdullah entered the ring, his forehead bearing battle scars so deep one could park a bicycle between the scabby grooves, fans knew that somebody's blood was sure to flow. At the end of a match, Abdullah usually stood, bloodied and victorious, with a sadistic gleam in his eye. Often he held a sharp object in his hand, smuggled into the ring when the referee was not looking. A fork was his favorite weapon.

Buddy "Nature Boy" Rogers becomes entangled in the ropes during a 1950 match with Lou Thesz. Unable to free himself, Rogers was counted out and had to rely on the referee to pry him loose.

ANDRE THE GIANT

Just one look at Andre the Giant was enough to convince anyone that he was aptly named. He stood 7' 5" and weighed 297 pounds. The "Eighth Wonder of the World," as he was known, was as strong as he appeared. A charging opponent would suddenly find himself hoisted into the air and thrown to the mat as if he weighed nothing.

Sudanese wrestler Abdullah "The Butcher" prepares to throw himself on Japan's Great Baba during a 1979 match in Chicago.

But André could also be gentle, as he showed when he starred in the movie, "The Princess Bride."

Born Andre Rene Roussimoff, Andre the Giant made his pro debut in 1964 in his native France. He rose to fame through a string of remarkable battle royal victories in Los Angeles in the early 1970s. Beloved by wrestling fans everywhere, he sold out arenas wherever he appeared. Undefeated for nearly 16 years, Andre captured more battle royal victories than any dozen other wrestlers combined. His complexities and winning ways made him the subject of one of the longest personal profiles in *Sports Illustrated* history.

In 1981 Killer Khan broke Andre's ankle, igniting one of the wildest feuds of the year. Seven years later, Andre shocked the wrestling world by turning against his fans and associating with rulebreakers. Andre hoped to secure a match against the popular Hulk Hogan for the world heavyweight title. Andre finally won the title in 1988. But two minutes after defeating Hogan, he sold his championship belt. World Wrestling Federation president Jack Tunney would later rule this transaction invalid.

In 1993, while in France to attend his father's funeral, Andre the Giant died of a heart attack.

VERN GAGNE

American pro wrestling in the 1960s and '70s was dominated by three major organizations: the National Wrestling Alliance (NWA), World Wrestling Federation (WWF), and American Wrestling Association (AWA). In the AWA, Vern Gagne was king.

Gagne brought an amateur sensibility to the pros that was as strong as his well-executed hammerlock. He was Big 10 champion four times in various weight classes at the University of Minnesota, where he also played football. He held three NCAA championships and won a spot on the 1948 U.S. Olympic team. Gagne turned pro in 1949. In 1969 he rose to national fame after being named the first AWA world champion. Gagne held this title nine times until his retirement in 1981. Although the AWA no longer exists, Vern Gagne's contributions to wrestling remain.

HARLEY RACE

Harley Race had a no-nonsense style to match his gravelly voice and steely-cold eyes. Race also had a lock on the National Wrestling Alliance world heavyweight title from 1977 to 1981. Race first wore NWA world championship gold on May 24, 1973, when he ended the four-year reign of Dory Funk Jr. Many fans believed the victory was a fluke, an opinion that grew stronger after Jack Brisco ended Race's reign after just two months.

It took four years for Race to regain that gold. But once he did, he made the belt his in a way that few champions have. During the next four years he spent just 22 days without the title. He wore the belt again in 1983; his six world heavyweight titles stand as a model of NWA excellence.

Harley Race wasn't flashy, but he got the job done. Sometimes he won with his signature piledriver, but more often he won through rugged determination. Harley had the kind of determination that often seemed to have been lost among a large contingent of grapplers who valued style over substance.

BRUNO SAMMARTINO

A native of Abruzzi, Italy, Bruno Sammartino made his pro debut in 1959, when Hulk Hogan was only 6 years old. Long before the "Hulkster" began to think about a wrestling career, Bruno Sammartino proved to the world why he truly deserved the nickname "The Living Legend."

On May 17, 1963, Bruno defeated "Nature Boy" Buddy Rogers in just 48 seconds to become the World Wrestling Federation world heavyweight champion. His title reign lasted a record 7 years. After losing to Ivan Koloff in 1971, Bruno came back to regain the title. This time he held it for 3 years. Between 1963 and 1977, Sammartino was the WWF champ for 11 of the 14 years, defeating every opponent who came his way.

Bruno's darkest hour came in April 1976, when Stan Hansen broke "The Living Legend's" neck in Madison Square Garden. Two months later, he made an astounding comeback, defeating Hansen in Shea Stadium as 42,000 fans cheered him on to victory.

Boxer Chuck Wepner is thrown from the ring by Andre the Giant in a rare boxer-wrestler match held at New York's Shea Stadium in 1976.

In 1991, *The Wrestler* magazine named Bruce Sammartino the most influential star of the preceding 25 years.

LOU THESZ

Professional wrestlers rate Lou Thesz among the greatest of all time. Thesz first won the NWA world heavyweight title by defeating Everett Marshall in December of 1937. He won it again from Marshall two years later. Then in 1947 he defeated Whipper Watson, and in 1948 he defeated Bill Lomgson, beginning a reign that lasted nearly eight years. He regained the title from Watson in 1956, held it for a year, and defeated Buddy Rogers in 1963 for a three-year reign.

Altogether, Lou Thesz held six NWA world titles over four decades. A superb mat technician in the ring and a gentleman out of the ring, Thesz won more than matches and titles. He won the respect of his peers in a sport that carried jealousy and distrust to the extreme. In 1990, Thesz wrestled one of his students, Masa Chono, in Japan. He lost, but still wrestled impressively—at the age of 74.

DUSTY RHODES

For five years after his 1969 pro debut, Dusty Rhodes was one of the most hated men in the sport. Not until 1974, when he turned against his manager, Gary Hart, did the fans turn to him. From then on, wrestling fans loved "The American Dream" almost as much as Rhodes loved the millions he called his "chillun'," the people on whose behalf he fought his battles. He won three heavyweight titles by defeating Ric Flair and twice defeating Harley Race.

But the longest of Dusty Rhodes's reigns was only three months. His wearing of the championship gold did not make him worthy of inclusion among the outstanding as much as his unique relationship with his fans. His popularity was built on the bionic elbow that sent many opponents down to defeat, and the boyish smile that could light up an arena filled with 20,000 fans. His interview style, in which he resembled Muhammad Ali wearing a John Deere cap, also made him popular. It all added up to a charisma that made this self-described "son of a plumber" one of the most popular wrestlers in history.

BUDDY ROGERS

Ric Flair may have made the nickname popular, but Buddy Rogers was the original "Nature Boy" of the squared circle.

Gorgeous George brought flamboyance to pro wrestling; Buddy Rogers brought attitude to the ring. His blond hair, arrogant strut, and condescending air caused millions to hate him. But Rogers had the bodybuilder's physique and enough athletic skills to capture and hold the NWA world heavyweight title from June 1961 to January 1963.

Roger's attitude made him a target of boxers as well as wrestlers. In 1959 the "Nature Boy" faced Jersey Joe Walcott in a memorable wrestler-boxer match.

After his retirement in the early 1980s, Rogers turned to management. He helped guide "Superfly" Jimmy Snuka to stardom in the early '80s, winning him the admiration of many of the fans who had previously despised him. By the time Rogers died in 1992, he had become one of the most beloved elder statesmen of the sport.

Frank Sexton has a footlock on Primo Carnera at a June 27, 1947, match, in the days before television and show business took over wrestling.

MIL MASCARAS

Some wrestling histories record that the first masked wrestler entered the ring in Paris in 1873 under the name of "The Masked Wrestler." Almost a century later, on December 18, 1972, the man many consider the greatest masked grappler of all time became the first disguised contestant to wrestle in Madison Square Garden.

Mil Mascaras—meaning 1,000 masks in Spanish—had made his pro debut in 1964. He often delighted the crowd by entering the ring and removing his colorful mask to reveal—not his face, but another mask. A popular movie star in his native Mexico, he wore a mask in all his films, too.

Mascaras possessed the physique, upper-body strength, fearlessness, and extensive knowledge of wrestling holds to excel as a wrestler. He used the flying bodypress off the top turnbuckle more than a decade before it became Jimmy "Superfly" Snuka's signature move.

3 THE WORLD CHAMPIONS

One of the most confusing things about professional wrestling is the fact that there is no one single champion of the sport. Unlike football, which crowns a Super Bowl winner each year, or baseball with its World Series, the world of wrestling is broken down into dozens of major and minor organizations, each with its own champion or group of title holders.

Some fans accept the claims of any federation that declares its title a "world title," while others take a more critical view, allowing that only the two or three largest federations can lay claim to holding world championships.

The 10 world champions profiled in this chapter are all athletes who have won the top singles titles in either the World Wrestling Federation or World Championship Wrestling (WCW), the two largest such groups in North America. Also profiled are the champions of the National Wrestling Alliance, the most influential North American organization until the early 1990s.

RIC FLAIR

Ric Flair is, in the eyes of many fans and fellow professionals, the best professional wrestler ever to lace up the boots. There have been many other wrestlers who were bigger or faster than the 6' 1", 243-pound Flair, with greater mobility and agility. Yet Flair dominated the field by winning 15 world titles in the three main organizations after turning pro in 1972.

Hulk Hogan and his co-star await the director's instructions while filming the comedy Rough Stuff, *in which Hogan plays a wrestler-turned-body-guard-turned-nanny.*

The supremely confident Ric Flair mastered the art of psychological warfare and preyed on the weaknesses in his opponent's mental game.

The genius of Flair lay in his mastery of the psychological side of the sport. He was able to detect and utilize every weak spot in his opponent's mental game. He knew that it took 100 percent confidence going into the ring and throughout the match to emerge a winner. Flair possessed supreme self-confidence, plus an arsenal of maneuvers, including his legendary figure-four leglock.

"Now we're going to school," he would scream with a grin as he clamped down on an unfortunate opponent.

TERRY FUNK

Terry Funk's NWA world title reign began on December 10, 1975, when he defeated Jack Brisco in Miami. He held the title until Harley Race defeated him in 1977.

Two decades later, years after his NWA rivals Brisco, Race, and Dusty Rhodes had retired, Funk was still snarling and swiping and slamming, making headlines in Extreme Championship Wrestling (ECW). Despite the violent and brutal nature of ECW matches, the 6' 1", 247-pound Funk was winning ECW heavyweight titles 32 years after his pro debut in 1965.

BRET HART

The 5' 11", 235-pound Bret Hart called himself "the best there is, the best there was, and the best there'll ever be." Many fans agreed with him.

One of several brothers, Bret grew up in Calgary, Alberta, under the watchful eye of his father, Stu, a former wrestler. With talents forged in their basement training room—"The Dungeon"—Bret rose to the top of the mat sport.

When Shawn Michaels ended Bret's third WWF reign at Wrestlemania XII on March 31, 1996, "The Hitman" Hart said he was retiring to spend time with his family. But a bidding war between the WWF and WCW resulted in the richest contract in the history of the sport. Offered a financial future that would guarantee

Hulk Hogan is in a head-lock given by "Macho Man" Randy Savage at the main event of Wrestlemania V, held in Atlantic City in 1989.

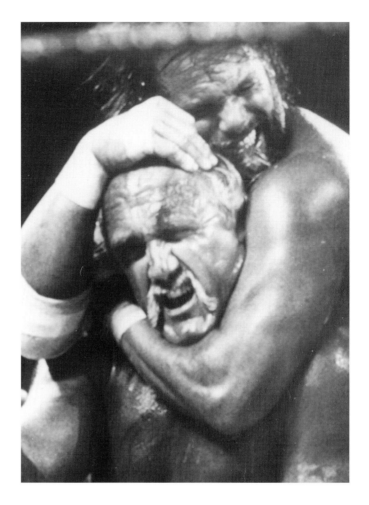

the comfort and education of his family, Hart signed a long-term contract with the WWF.

HULK HOGAN

January 23, 1984, stands as one of the watershed dates in wrestling history. On that cool night in New York's Madison Square Garden, Hulk Hogan took just five minutes and 40 seconds to dismantle the Iron Sheik, claim the WWF world heavyweight title, and launch the worldwide frenzy known as Hulkamania.

Over the next few years, the 6'8", 275-pound Hogan was the foundation upon which grew a new era of pro wrestling: Wrestlemania extravaganzas, pay-per-view events, and mainstream media coverage. Hogan appeared on the covers of *Sports Illustrated* and *MAD* magazine, hosted Saturday Night Live, and appeared on MTV. He had a role in "Rocky III" and starred in several movies.

Hogan earned the credit for making pro wrestling popular, but the sport had always drawn enormous crowds. Hogan's accomplishment was to elevate wrestling in the eyes of the media and other businesses. Because of him, wrestling merchandise deals began to happen in unprecedented ways: wrestling toys, dolls, and videogames appeared. Thanks to Hulkamania, the action spread beyond the ring to toy stores and corporate boardrooms.

Never considered a superior technical wrestler, Hogan used his big foot to the head followed by a thundering legdrop to win several world titles. Then, in the late 1990s, Hogan turned against the fans and the WWF that had made him a worldwide celebrity and a multimillionaire. As leader of the renegade New World Order (NWO) in WCW, Hogan was set to close out his career as one of the most hated men in the sport.

As favorite or villain, Hulk Hogan made a lasting impression on the world of wrestling.

LEX LUGER

When Lex Luger made his pro debut on Halloween night 1985, those in attendance must have wondered whether they were looking at some sort of elaborate costume. His 6'5", 265-pound frame carried layer upon layer of muscle, a confident attitude, and a pair of eyes burning with intensity of purpose.

Less than a month later, Luger won his first championship, a regional title in Florida, and the wrestling world paid attention to "The Total Package."

In addition to a WCW world title, Luger held the NWA/WCW U.S. heavyweight title four times, and the WCW world tag team title once with his best friend, Sting. Yet for all the championship gold he had worn, fans did not seem satisfied with his efforts. The term "unrealized potential" hounded him, despite the titles and acclaim he earned.

SHAWN MICHAELS

In a sport that values flamboyance more than athleticism, Shawn Michaels managed to excel in both. In the latter half of the 1990s, the 6', 234-pound Michaels was a superior athlete at the top of his form. In addition to a WWF world title, he had won two consecutive Royal Rumbles, 30-man endurance contests that required the utmost in stamina and ability. His success won him the number one ranking by *Pro Wrestling Illustrated* (PWI) for 1996.

Whether or not a title was at stake, Michaels always put forth a spectacular effort. Superb at both scientific wrestling and brawling, Michaels was involved in PWI Match of the Year winners for four years in a row.

RANDY SAVAGE

The 6'2", 237-pound "Macho Man" Randy Savage wore silly outfits and gave dull interviews when he first turned pro in 1973. But once he removed the giant hat and funky sunglasses and the opening bell rang, Savage's killer instinct came to the fore. A four-time world title holder, Savage joined with Hulk Hogan to form the Megapowers in the late 1980s. Later they traded in the fan adoration of the Megapowers for the renegade attitude of the NWO.

STING

Sting's first big match took place on March 27, 1988, about three years after he had made his pro debut. The next morning the nation was buzzing about the new face-painted phenomenon who had taken "Nature Boy" Ric Flair to a 45-minute draw on national television at Clash of the Champions I. In those 45 minutes, Sting made the transition from a regional star to an international superstar. With charisma to spare, he became as popular in the NWA and WCW as Hulk Hogan was in the WWF.

The 6'2", 260-pound Sting went into matches and interviews alike with unbridled enthusiasm. His face paint always changed. His in-ring tactics, featuring the "Stinger splash" and "scorpion leglock," brought cheering fans to their feet.

Talent and momentum drove Sting to the top. He won two world titles and mobilized millions of fans. His army of "little Stingers" almost matched Hogan's legion of "Hulkamaniacs."

In the late 1990s Sting's face paint lost its color. His enthusiasm gave way to dark moodiness. Sting was undergoing a change that could determine not only his future but the character of the wrestling scene as well—darker personalities took center stage as the 20th century drew to a close.

Undertaker poses during a press conference held in 1997 to publicize New Jersey's elimination of the media tax on televised professional wrestling events.

THE UNDERTAKER

Standing 6' 9" and weighing 328 pounds, The Undertaker projected the fear of death onto his opponents. His massive physique gave him physical dominance and the ability to absorb punishment meted out by his foes. Lacking the scientific skills of other stars, he still won two WWF world titles by defeating Hulk Hogan and Sid Vicious.

VADER

The moonsault, a popular maneuver among lightweight wrestlers, was carried to another level when the 450-pound Vader launched it. His opponent, lying groggy on the canvas, saw the back of a large hulking figure scaling the turnbuckles in the corner of the ring. The masked Vader then hoisted himself to the top turnbuckle. With a few trampoline-like bounces on the ropes, he hurled his hefty bulk into the air, turned a backward somersault and landed on his victim with a splat that shook the canvas and the entire arena.

Vader combined incredible agility for a man so big with a vicious attitude to inflict his pain game on anyone who challenged him.

4 CHAMPIONSHIP GOLD

In addition to world titles, most wrestling organizations feature secondary titles. The World Wrestling Federation, for example, has an Intercontinental title. World Championship Wrestling has a U.S. heavyweight title. Smaller groups have their own significant championships. The ECW (Extreme Championship Wrestling) heavyweight title and USWA (United States Wrestling Association) have their own crowns.

The 10 wrestlers profiled in this chapter have all worn championship gold, although not generally in the world champion class.

GOLDUST

Casual fans know him as a bizarre Hollywood-obsessed individual covered in gold paint. Longtime fans know that beneath the makeup, Goldust is actually Dustin Rhodes, the son of legendary three-time NWA world champion Dusty Rhodes.

Dustin, a native of Austin, Texas, was a rugged cowboy-booted grappler in the style of his father and other Texas stars such as Dick Murdoch and the Funks. But the 6'5", 254-pound Goldust enjoyed creating an image. He covered himself in gold body paint and delivered interviews that consisted mostly of quotes from old movies.

Roddy Piper prepares to be slammed onto the mat by Hulk Hogan during the 1985 Wrestlemania at New York's Madison Square Garden.

SCOTT HALL

A big man with a big attitude, the 6'8", 299-pound Scott Hall held the now-defunct American Wrestling Association world tag team title for four months in 1986. That was the biggest achievement of his career, until he decided that Scott Hall was someone who needed to be replaced.

Hall became Razor Ramon. With a swaggering Latino image as imposing as his massive physique, Ramon dominated the WWF Intercontinental field, defeating formidable

After winning three WWF Intercontinental titles, Jeff Jarett experimented with a country music career, then returned to join World Championship Wrestling.

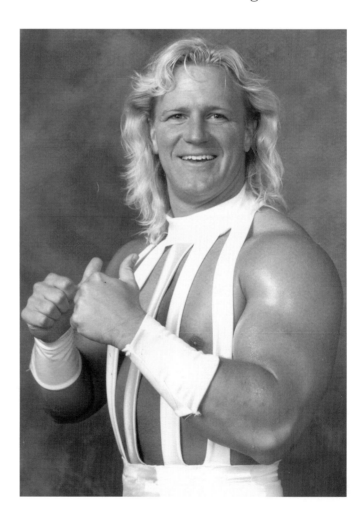

opponents Rick Martel, Diesel, Jeff Jarett, and Dean Douglas.

Then along came the New World Order, which revitalized competition in World Championship Wrestling. Hall shed the Razor Ramon act and resumed wrestling under his own name.

JEFF JARRETT

When Jeff Jarrett left Memphis, Tennessee, where he had built a following for nearly a decade, the 5'10", 230-pound grappler won three WWF Intercontinental titles. Then he left the ring to try his luck in a country music career. When that faltered, Jarrett joined World Championship Wrestling.

An accomplished singles wrestler, Jarrett was equally at home in tag team matches. A scientific wrestler, he could also become a brawler, taking the action out of the ring when the occasion demanded.

JERRY LAWLER

The king of Memphis wrestling expanded his realm to include the World Wrestling Federation, but longtime fans remembered when Lawler's attitude brought him national attention.

Lawler and comedian Andy Kaufman appeared on "Late Night With David Letterman" on July 29, 1982. They engaged in a shouting match that ended with Kaufman throwing hot coffee in Lawler's face. Kaufman agreed to wrestle Lawler in Memphis, where the professional wrestler gave the comedian a wrestling lesson that landed the entertainer in a neckbrace.

Lawler's decades-long dominance of the USWA scene in Memphis led to WWF matches and feuds that won him a national audience, most of whom hated him. But it did not matter to Lawler how the fans felt about him, as long as they didn't ignore him.

MARC MERO

Marc Mero began his career as Johnny B. Badd, a flamboyant performer dressed in pink, with a verbal style that was a cross between boxer Muhammad Ali and rocker Little Richard.

As Johnny B. Badd, he captured attention in WCW circles. Some of it derived from the heavy eyeliner he painted on his face and the confetti he threw into the audience prior to each match, but most of it came from his spectacular aerial maneuvers, including one of the best sunset flips the sport has ever seen.

After establishing himself in WCW, Mero shed the wild outfits and brash attitude in favor of a more conservative approach. He moved to the WWF, used his real name, and adopted a no-nonsense approach that emphasized substance over style.

Mero turned pro in 1991, and he had won one Intercontinental title by the late 1990s.

KEVIN NASH

The 7', 356-pound Kevin Nash turned pro in 1990. He entered the WWF early in 1994 as a bodyguard to Shawn Michaels. Before long, he had captured the WWF tag team title with Michaels, an Intercontinental title, and the WWF world title under the name Diesel.

Seeking more control over his career, Nash moved to WCW, and joined with Scott Hall in forming NWO. They were later joined by Hulk Hogan.

RODDY PIPER

Roddy Piper's longevity in the sport is astonishing, considering his intense and brutal ring style. On November 24, 1983, Piper battled Greg Valentine at Starrcade '83 in a dog-collar chain match. The two men wore collars connected by a steel chain in a brutal and bloody bout that saw Piper emerge with severe ear damage.

The relatively small 6' 2" Piper prides himself on being able to brawl with the biggest. In addition to his WCW action, Piper has appeared in movies.

RICK RUDE

Rick Rude has wrestled and captured championships in both the WWF and WCW, infuriating fans and top stars ever since he turned pro in 1983.

The 6' 4", 246-pound wrestler perfected a unique prematch routine. He entered the ring to bump-and-grind theme music, then grabbed the microphone and screamed, "Cut the music." He then unleashed a stream of insults at the fans in the arena, whipping their anger and hatred into a wave of noisy rebuttal.

"Hit the music," he commanded as he disrobed, drawing attention to his washboard stomach. He then turned and pummeled his opponent who was standing in the ring awaiting the opening bell.

DAVEY BOY SMITH

A native of Leeds, England, Davey Boy Smith was wrestling nationally for nearly a decade before garnering his first taste of national fame as part of the British Bulldogs

After losing his world champion belt in 1990, Hulk Hogan points to the new WWF champion, Ultimate Warrior.

tag team with Dynamite Kid. The team held the WWF tag team title in 1986 and '87. Then, as often happens with tag teams, injuries and dreams of individual glory broke them apart. Smith went on to take the WWF Intercontinental title from Bret Hart, his reign lasting only two months before Shawn Michaels took it from him. Only 5' 9" and 245 pounds, Smith then teamed with Lex Luger for a while, switching between singles and team competition.

ULTIMATE WARRIOR

On April 1, 1990, at Wrestlemania VI, the Ultimate Warrior defeated Hulk Hogan in 22 minutes, 51 seconds to capture the WWF heavyweight title. The match involved two fan favorites, a rarity in the world of highly-charged feuds. As Hogan left the ring to return to his dressing room, he turned and faced the two-time Intercontinental champion who had defeated him and raised his right arm in a salute to Warrior's victory. Warrior responded in kind.

The Warrior's face paint, his hyper ring entrances, and his 6' 3", 280-pound stature made him popular. Thousands of fans mobbed him wherever he appeared; sales of his merchandise were second to those of Hulk Hogan. Warrior's career, however, peaked in 1990.

5 THE TAG TEAMS

Wrestling is basically a singles sport, one man taking on another relying on nothing but skills and wits. Tag team wrestling consists of teams of two on a side, but only one pair of opponents battle at a time. Partners switch by tagging each other. Tag team matches were banned in many states for the first half of the twentieth century. New York lifted its ban in 1953. As tag teams began competing in Madison Square Garden, their popularity grew.

Since then, tag team wrestling has risen and fallen in popularity, depending on the personalities of teams that come and go. All the teams profiled in this chapter have made significant contributions not only to tag team wrestling, but to the sport of wrestling itself.

THE FOUR HORSEMEN

More than a tag team of two wrestlers, the four Horsemen was a mix-and-match quartet. With Ric Flair as its focus, the Four Horsemen dominated the National Wrestling Alliance and World Championship Wrestling for much of the 1990s.

The Horsemen formed in May of 1986, originally consisting of Flair, Tully Blanchard, Arn Anderson, Ole Anderson, and manager James J. Dillon. Through the years the membership changed, sometimes adding Sting and Lex Luger. Despite the changes, they often held more than one title at the same time.

The Road Warriors, also called the "Legion of Doom," are known for wearing face paint, leather, and spikes.

THE FREEBIRDS

In the 1980s Michael "P.S." Hayes, Terry "Bam Ram" Gordy, and Buddy "Jack" Roberts formed the toughest wrestling cooperative in the sport. From the Carolinas to Texas, the Freebirds distinguished themselves with a hard-nosed wrestling style in the ring and hard-partying attitude out of the ring.

While Vince McMahon and the WWF may be credited with boosting the rock and wrestling connection, the Freebirds took it to a new level, using Lynyrd Skynyrd's "Freebird" as their entrance music.

The Freebirds were involved in a years-long feud that began on Christmas night in 1982. Kerry Von Erich was battling National Wrestling Alliance world champion Ric Flair in a steel cage in Dallas with Michael Hayes (later known as Dok Hendrix in the WWF) as special referee. Von Erich and Flair were both dazed after a mid-ring collision. Hayes put Von Erich on top of the champ, but Von Erich refused to win the belt that way. Hayes called him an idiot; as Von Erich left the ring, Hayes's partner, Terry Gordy, slammed the cage door shut on Von Erich's head. The incident was the first shot fired in a war that embroiled Texas wrestling fans for five years.

HARLEM HEAT

Hailing from the mean streets of Harlem in New York, Booker T (5' 11", 250 pounds) and Stevie Ray (6' 1", 265 pounds) blended muscles and acrobatic maneuvers to win seven WCW world tag team titles. Along the way they defeated duos such as The Nasty Boys, Rick and Scott Steiner, and Lex Luger and Sting.

A successful combination of acrobat and athlete, Booker T and Stevie Ray of Harlem Heat have won seven WCW world tag team titles.

Their first WCW title reign began in 1994 and their seventh title reign ended in 1996 when they were defeated by Scott Hall and Kevin Nash. In the two years between 1994 and 1996, Harlem Heat spent only about eight months without the championship gold around their waists.

THE HART FOUNDATION

Before Bret "The Hitman" Hart distinguished himself as a singles champion and signed the richest contract in wrestling history—a 20-year deal with the WWF—he was

Dennis Rodman looks tiny compared to the Giant, who has him in a choke hold at his WCW debut.

a member of The Hart Foundation, a tag team that included his brother-in-law, Jim "The Anvil" Neidhart.

The Hart Foundation first rose to world tag team champions on January 26, 1987, when they defeated the British Bulldogs. Nine months later they lost the title to Ric Martel and Tito Santana, but they regained it in 1990 by whipping Demolition at the WWF Summerslam.

Led by Hart's "sharpshooter" leglock, The Hart Foundation earned fans' respect with a no-nonsense approach to the mat wars.

THE MIDNIGHT EXPRESS

The Midnight Express was by far the most formidable duo in the sport throughout the 1980s. First Dennis Condrey and Bobby Eaton, then Eaton and Stan Lane combined with their manager, Jim Cornette, to develop a finely-tuned machine that delivered rapid-fire maneuvers in the ring, and surreptitious rule-breaking outside the ring.

Condrey and Eaton held the National Wrestling Alliance world tag team title for six months in 1986, while Eaton and Lane held the belts for about six weeks in 1988.

THE NASTY BOYS

Brian Knobs and Jerry Sags grew up on the streets of Allentown, Pennsylvania, and became two of the roughest, meanest wrestlers in the sport. Knobs and Sags were as likely to smash an opponent over the head with a garbage pail as crush them in the face with a fist. They scrapped their way to a WWF title in 1991 and three WCW world tag team titles between 1993 and 1995.

THE ROAD WARRIORS

The Road Warriors redefined tag team wrestling when they made their debut in 1983, with face paint and meanness. Hawk and Animal, faces painted and their bodies clad in spikes and leather, came into the ring amid a deafening thunder of heavy metal power chords.

Basketball star Dennis Rodman spray paints a wrestler's back in victory while his tag team partner, Hulk Hogan, watches.

Managed by Paul Ellering, the "Legion of Doom," as they were known, established themselves as the meanest boys on the block. Everyone wanted to defeat them, but few could. After winning the Georgia National tag team title, they claimed belts in the American Wrestling Association, National Wrestling Alliance, and World Wrestling Federation between 1984 and 1992.

They also made their mark in the competitive Japanese pro ranks, and became the only duo to be voted Tag Team of the Year for three years (1983–1985) by the readers of

Pro Wrestling Illustrated magazine. Hawk and Animal, as everyone (even their families) call them, have been part of the same tag team for 14 years and have a rock-solid relationship—a rarity in the wrestling world, where feuds and salary disputes often break up tag teams.

THE ROCK 'N' ROLL EXPRESS

Rick Morton and Robert Gibson burst on the wrestling scene in the mid-1980s with a style that nobody had seen before. They blended teen magazine looks with a fast-paced, quick-tag acrobatic style that confounded opponents, especially their arch-rivals, The Midnight Express.

Morton and Gibson won their first National Wrestling Alliance world tag team title on July 9, 1985, defeating Ivan Koloff and Krusher Krushchev. That reign lasted just three months, but three more NWA title reigns followed over the next two years.

For a brief time Morton set out on his own in an effort to win the NWA heavyweight title, but he soon returned to the team. The Rock 'n' Roll Express were often copied, especially by The Midnight Rockers (Shawn Michaels and Marty Jannetty) in the erstwhile American Wrestling Association.

THE STEINERS

When the massively muscled Scott Steiner signaled to the crowd, they knew what to expect: Scott was about to hurl his opponent into the ropes. On the rebound, he jumped into the air and wrapped his powerful legs around his opponent's head, then snapped his body to the mat. Scott then flipped his foe over in a lightning-fast move that always spelled victory.

The move was called the Frankensteiner. Scott teamed with his brother, Rick, to create the Steinerliner. As Scott hoisted a foe upon his shoulders, Rick climbed to the top turn-buckle and delivered a flying clothesline.

The Steiners won NWA and WCW world tag team titles four times and the WWF belts twice. They also excelled in Japan.

THE VON ERICHS

The Von Erichs, a family of popular wrestlers, could have been one of wrestling's greatest success stories. Instead, they are the sport's greatest tragedy. Of the five wrestling Von Erichs—David, Kerry, Kevin, Mike, and Chris—four died young. Three of the four took their own lives. In addition, their oldest brother, Jack Jr., died in an accident on the family's Texas farm in 1959.

Though their name is Adkisson, the family became known to the wrestling world as the Von Erichs. Father Fritz Von Erich (born Jack Adkisson) was a football star and wrestler. He later became a wrestling promoter and created World Class Wrestling, a syndicated wrestling show based in Dallas, Texas. World Class Wrestling ran for years and was seen in the U.S., Japan, Argentina, and the Middle East. Fritz Von Erich hoped that his sons would help him in promoting wrestling entertainment.

With five talented boys, the Von Erich family looked like a wrestling dynasty to many wrestling fans. David Von Erich became a wrestler first, forging a path for his brothers to follow. By the 1980s, the five Von Erich brothers had become internationally recognized in the sport, winning championship belts in the U.S. and abroad. The Von Erichs, who always filled the arenas where they were competing, even wrestled at Texas stadium, before a crowd of 40,000.

Then, in 1984, while on tour in Japan, David Von Erich died from an intestinal inflammation. The family bounced back from that loss. Brother Kerry Von Erich, once an Olympic-hopeful discus thrower, went on to win the NWA world heavyweight championship by defeating Rick Flair in May of 1984. Later he won a WWF International championship.

Just a few years after his brother Kerry's victories, Mike Von Erich became seriously ill from toxic shock syndrome. The illness, which nearly killed him, forced him to give up his wrestling career. Depressed, he overdosed on tranquilizers and died. The death of three of his brothers was too much for Chris Von Erich, who was struggling with his own shaky wrestling career. Distraught, Chris Von Erich took his own life in 1991.

The tragedy of the Von Erich family continued. In 1986, Kerry Von Erich, the family star, had lost a foot in a motorcycle accident. He later became addicted to painkillers. After facing charges of forging prescriptions for painkillers and of drug possession, Kerry also chose to take his own life.

Now 40 years old, Kevin Von Erich is the only surviving Von Erich son. His father, Fritz, died of cancer in September 1997.

6 — BEYOND 2000

As pro wrestling neared the year 2000, it underwent many changes. The World Wrestling Federation, which had dominated the field for about 10 years, met significant competition from World Championship Wrestling, which was controlled by the Time-Warner Corporation. Smaller federations, such as Extreme Championship Wrestling, drew some of wrestling's worldwide fans. The flash and glitter that had marked the sport gave way to a more brutal style of wrestling that emphasized technical moves and high-risk aerial maneuvers. No-holds barred competitions like Ultimate Fighting drew wrestlers who were eager to prove their skills outside the wrestling arena.

Wrestlers were expected to back up their boasts with skills so they could compete against a variety of opponents and types of attacks. Psychological warfare became widely employed. To appeal to audiences in this new era of wrestling, some wrestlers adopted darker personalities.

This chapter profiles 10 who could survive and thrive in the 21st century.

STEVE AUSTIN

The name "Stone Cold" Steve Austin fits this shaved-head, steely-gazed competitor, whose demeanor and ring presence are icy and brutal. The 6'2", 241-pound Austin is an extremely focused wrestler, concentrating his skills and

At an intimidating 7'4"—just one inch shorter than the late wrestling great Andre the Giant—the Giant has propelled himself to popularity.

ability on dismantling his opponent in any way possible. A technician as well as an all-out brawler, Austin is often compared with the young Ric Flair. Austin has competed in World Championship Wrestling, Extreme Championship Wrestling, and in the World Wrestling Federation. He won the 1996 King of the Ring award and the 1997 Royal Rumble.

Austin was not always a solo star. At first, his future seemed to lie in tag team action. He and Brian Pillman appeared as The Hollywood Blonds and held the WCW tag team title for much of 1993. But their clashing egos made long-term cooperation impossible. As is the case with many tag team partnerships, they split up to pursue solo careers.

THE GIANT

When Andre the Giant died in 1993, the sport thought it would never see anything like him again. Then came The Giant. Only an inch shorter than Andre at 7'4" and weighing 430 pounds, The Giant proved to be a worthy competitor. Despite his size, he is both agile and skilled, two qualities that enabled him to become the first rookie in pro wrestling history to capture the WCW world title. The Giant won the title after he defeated Ric Flair on April 22, 1996. He held the title until August 10, 1996, when he lost it to Hulk Hogan.

In a sport where wrestlers tend to take eight to ten years of pro action to make their mark, The Giant had an immediate impact on the mat world.

EDDY GUERRERO

Relatively small at 5'8" and 221 pounds, Eddy Guerrero brought excitement to the World

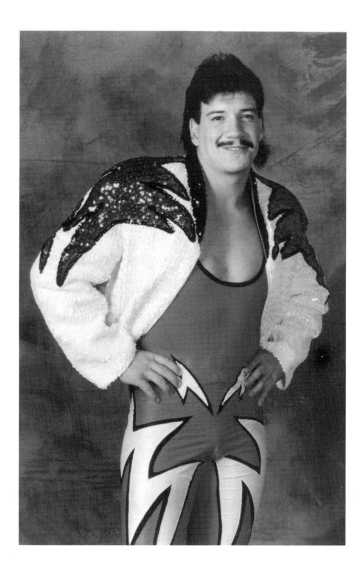

Although smaller than most professional wrestlers, Eddie Guerrero is a reckless and dangerous opponent who has climbed to the top ranks of Extreme Championship Wrestling.

Championship Wrestling cruiserweight division, winning the WCW World Cruiserweight title in 1997. He also became a top star in the brutal arena of Extreme Championship Wrestling. Guerrero blends a technical mastery of complex mat holds with a fearless, even reckless willingness to hurl his body through the air in high-risk, high-impact maneuvers. As a result, Guerrero quickly became a favorite among wrestling fans who cared more for the action inside the ring than for the bravado at the broadcasters' table.

In all of his matches, Guerrero faces two foes: his opponent in the ring, and the fear that he could cripple himself with his next maneuver.

AHMED JOHNSON

Ahmed Johnson, whose real name is Tony Norris, was named the WWF Rookie of the Year in 1995. Johnson was the first wrestler to slam Yokozuna at 641 pounds. A native of Mississippi and former NFL player, Johnson is considered one of the strongest wrestlers in the WWF. In a 1996 WWF match against Farooq, Ahmed Johnson suffered a lacerated kidney. Doctors doubted that he would ever wrestle again. But six months later Johnson was back in the title wars of the WWF, hoping to become the first black world heavyweight champion.

The injury was the low point of a 1996 that was packed with high points for this 6'2", 305-pound athlete. The year included an Intercontinental title victory over Goldust at the WWF King of the Ring on June 23. The injury forced Johnson to vacate the title. But Johnson refused to let it deter his drive to be a champion.

DEAN MALENKO

It took years, but 5'9", 216-pound Dean Malenko finally achieved recognition as the best mat technician in the world. The son of noted rulebreaker Boris Malenko, Dean toiled in the background as Hulkamania reigned

Known as the "Man of 1,000 Holds," Dean Malenko is widely considered to be one of the most accomplished and skilled wrestlers in the world.

supreme in the 1980s. Fans were enthralled more by personality and style and flash and glitter by than substance.

Then the pendulum swung back, and skilled athletes like Malenko, the "Man of

1,000 Holds," drew more attention. Malenko won the WCW cruiserweight title in 1996, giving his technical approach to the sport more prominence and recognition. Malenko's success helped scientific wrestling to become more popular with fans and other wrestlers.

MANKIND

Mankind, who was known as Cactus Jack or Cactus Jack Manson before he re-invented himself, is willing to absorb incredible amounts of punishment in order to punish his foe. He once somersaulted out of the ring onto the concrete floor in an effort to inflict harm to an opponent.

Inflicting damage is his objective, even if it costs him suffering in the process. On March 16, 1994, he lost two-thirds of an ear to Vader during a match in Germany.

There are few things that demonstrate the 6' 4", 277-pound Mankind's bizarre approach to the sport better than his finishing hold known as the mandible claw. Mankind reaches into his opponent's throat and chokes him from the inside.

DALLAS PAGE

When Scott Hall wrestled as the Diamond Studd in the 1990s, Dallas Page was his manager. When Studd left WCW to compete in the WWF as Razor Ramon, Page was left with nobody to manage. So he decided to manage himself.

The 6' 5", 260-pound Page made the rare transition from manager to successful wrestler. Since winning a WCW title in 1995, he has become focused on winning the heavyweight title. His "diamond cutter" finishing maneuver may be more effective than that of Jake "The Snake" Roberts, who first made the move popular. In the maneuver, Page faces his opponent, who is bent at the waist. Page grabs the man's head in the crook of his arm, then falls backward, slamming his opponent's forehead into the canvas.

BRIAN PILLMAN

A former NFL player with the Cincinnati Bengals, Brian Pillman, or "Flyin' Brian," as he was known, distinguished himself quickly in the pro ranks as a superb technician and a fearless practitioner of aerial maneuvers. As a member of The Hollywood Blonds tag team with Steve Austin, Pillman held the World Championship Wrestling World tag team title for five months in 1993. Then the partnership broke up. Pillman's attitude grew darker, his actions unpredictable. But that change revitalized his career, first in Extreme Championship Wrestling, then in the World Wrestling Federation. Pillman appeared to have what it takes to succeed in wrestling.

Then, in October of 1997, Brain Pillman was found dead in his hotel room. He was only 35 years old. His death shocked family, friends, fans, and other wrestlers. Some in the industry believed Pillman had been suffering ever since injuries sustained in a car accident forced him to rely on painkillers in order to continue his career. Bret Hart, a friend who was traveling with Pillman at the time of his death, published an insightful article in the *Calgary Sun* that spoke of the pressures that he and other wrestlers face.

According to Hart, "You look for ways to endure the physical pain of a broken body and hope you don't become so numb that you end up with a broken spirit. In the ring, you're a superhero and you search down deep inside to make that strength real. It's dangerous to forget that even Superman had his kryptonite . . . The business killed Brian Pillman and it could have been any one of us."

RAVEN

In Extreme Championship Wrestling, violence and brutality are the order of the day. Any competitor who rises to the top must be able to inflict and withstand a great deal of punishment.

In 1996, Raven won the Extreme Championship Wrestling heavyweight title twice, defeating The Sandman both times. Quiet, intense, and methodical, Raven's strategies are timeless: throw an opponent off balance with pre-match psychological warfare, then do whatever is necessary to win the match. Win or lose, Raven never expresses any pleasure or joy in the outcome. His ring presence is always cold and emotionless.

TAZ

Standing 5' 11" and weighing 221 pounds, Taz is a mass of solid muscle, Taz takes his name from the cartoon figure, the Tasmanian Devil. Like the Tasmanian Devil, Taz is a whirlwind of energy. He enters the ring and assaults his foes with a tornado-like fury.

Like his competitor, Raven, Taz also rose to prominence in Extreme Championship

Wrestling. His stable of maneuvers runs toward suplexes—body-snapping, bone-jarring moves that can quickly win a match or inflict injury on an opponent.

Eager to prove his toughness and his versatility, Taz has challenged competitors outside the mat sport. In 1996, he took on Ultimate Fighting's Paul Varelans.

20 HISTORIC MOMENTS

January 18, 1971	"Russian Bear" Ivan Koloff ends the 7-year reign of WWF champion "Living Legend" Bruno Sammartino at New York's Madison Square Garden.
June 25, 1976	Japanese wrestling legend Antonio Inoki battles boxing super-star Muhammad Ali to a 15-round draw in a rare wrestler vs. boxer contest. The match, held before 32,000 fans in New York's Shea Stadium, is broadcast live to a worldwide audience via closed-circuit television.
August 9, 1980	Bruno Sammartino defeats his former student, Larry Zbyszko, in a steel cage match that drew more than 40,000 fans to New York's Shea Stadium.
November 24, 1983	In the main event of the Starrcade '83 extravaganza, "Nature Boy" Ric Flair captures his second National Wrestling Alliance world title from Harley Race; it is the first time in the title's eight-decade history that the belt has changed hands inside a steel cage.
January 23, 1984	Hulk Hogan dismantles the Iron Sheik in five minutes 40 seconds at New York's Madison Square Garden to capture the WWF world title and signal the official beginning of Hulkamania—and the modern wrestling era.
March 31, 1995	The first Wrestlemania card is held, drawing an estimated closed-circuit audience of 400,000 fans and setting a new standard for megapromotions in the modern era. In the main event, WWF World champion Hulk Hogan and Mr. T defeat "Mr. Wonderful" Paul Orndorff and "Rowdy" Roddy Piper.
May 11, 1985	NBC broadcasts the WWF's Saturday Night's Main Event program, marking the return of professional wrestling to network television for the first time in 30 years.
November 7, 1985	Wrestling's first pay-per-view card, the WWF Wrestling Classic, is held at the Rosemont Horizon in Chicago.

20 HISTORIC MOMENTS

March 29, 1987   A North American pro wrestling attendance record is
set as more than 93,000 fans flock to the Pontiac Silverdome
in Pontiac, Michigan, to witness the WWF's Wrestlemania III
pay-per-view card. In the main event, WWF World champion
Hulk Hogan defeated Andre the Giant.

November 1988   Atlanta-based media mogul Ted Turner purchases Jim
Crockett Promotions, the largest member of the National
Wrestling Alliance, and renames the organization World
Championship Wrestling.

December 26, 1990   At the age of 74, six-time National Wrestling Alliance
champion Lou Thesz—who won his first NWA title in
1937—wrestles impressively against 27-year-old Masa Chono,
one of his own students, at a card in Hamamatsu, Japan.

September 10, 1991   The wrestling world is shocked as "Nature Boy" Ric Flair—
a mainstay of the National Wrestling Alliance and World
Championship Wrestling—makes his debut in the WWF;
he returns to WCW in February 1993.

April 25, 1992   "Superfly" Jimmy Snuka defeats "Wildman" Bellomo in
Philadelphia to become the first-ever ECW champion.
Initially known as Eastern Championship Wrestling, the
organization became Extreme Championship Wrestling
on August 27, 1994, and set new standards for violence
and brutality.

September 2, 1992   Andre the Giant makes his last appearance on U.S.
television during the live broadcast of World Championship
Wrestling's "Clash of the Champions" aired on TBS; a few
months later, on January 27, 1993, Andre the Giant died.

November 18, 1993   WWF head Vince McMahon is indicted on charges of
possession of anabolic steroids and conspiracy to
distribute anabolic steroids. He is acquitted of all charges
on July 22, 1994.

20 HISTORIC MOMENTS

June 11, 1994   The wrestling world is stunned when WWF icon
Hulk Hogan signs with the WWF's arch-rival, World
Championship Wrestling.

April 29, 1995   Pro wrestling enjoys its largest live attendance ever as
190,000 fans witness a card at Mayday Stadium in Pyongyang,
North Korea. In the main event clash of two legendary
stars, Japanese sensation Antonio Inoki defeats "Nature Boy"
Ric Flair.

September 4, 1995   World Championship Wrestling debuts WCW Monday Nitro,
a live program intended to compete with the WWF's live
broadcast of WWF Monday Night Raw.

December 16, 1995   Though the once-mighty National Wrestling Alliance dwindled
to near obscurity, the NWA championship continued to be
a model of pro wrestling's superiority among world athletes
as NWA champion Dan Severn captured the UFC Ultimate
Ultimate championship. Eight months earlier, on April 8, 1995,
Severn had captured the Ultimate Fight V championship.

July 7, 1996   The New World Order, a renegade group of "outsiders" that
declared war on World Championship Wrestling, is officially
formed. Charter members included Scott Hall, Kevin Nash,
and Hulk Hogan.

FURTHER READING

Jares, Joe. *Whatever Happened to Gorgeous George?* Englewood Cliffs,
     New Jersey: Prentice Hall, 1974.

Lentz, Harris M. Biographical *Dictionary of Professional Wrestling.*
     Jefferson, N.C.: McFarland, 1996.

Morgan, Roberta. *The Main Event: The World of Pro Wrestling.*
     New York: Dial Press, 1971.

Myers, Robert. *The Professional Wrestling Trivia Book.*
     Brookline, MA: Branden Co., 1988.

Sandelson, Robert. *Combat Sports.* Morristown, N.J.:
     Silver Burdett, 1991.

INDEX

PICTURE CREDITS Library of Congress: p. 2; New York Public Library: pp. 6, 8, 9, 58; AP/Wide World Photos: pp. 10, 12, 15, 20, 24, 28, 30, 42, 44; Archive Photos, 18, 36; World Championship Wrestling, 22, 32, 41, 48, 51, 53; World Wrestling Federation, 38

MATT HUNTER has spent more than a dozen years in the professional wrestling business—on the road, in front of and behind the television cameras, in the locker rooms, behind the scenes, and on the newsstands. In addition to this book on pro wrestling, the author has written newspaper and magazine articles on topics as varied as music and politics, authored dozens of video game instruction manuals, crafted a wide variety of advertising and public relations materials for print and broadcast, and developed content for interactive media. He lives in Pennsylvania.

ACKNOWLEDGMENTS
Thanks to DG and DB for the gig … to PK for the original callback … to SW for fair treatment … to BA, SS, and SF for lifelong friendships and the establishment of professional standards far too high for the current regime … to BP for the ticket out … and to all the rest—NK, DM, and those far too numerous to mention—as CF so frequently and elegantly said: "They know who they are!"